IT'S TIME TO EAT SWEET POTATO FRIES

It's Time to Eat SWEET POTATO FRIES

Walter the Educator

Silent King Books
A WhichHead Entertainment Imprint

Disclaimer

This book is a literary work; the story is not about specific persons, locations, situations, and/or circumstances unless mentioned in a historical context. Any resemblance to real persons, locations, situations, and/or circumstances is coincidental. This book is for entertainment and informational purposes only. The author and publisher offer this information without warranties expressed or implied. No matter the grounds, neither the author nor the publisher will be accountable for any losses, injuries, or other damages caused by the reader's use of this book. The use of this book acknowledges an understanding and acceptance of this disclaimer.

It's Time to Eat SWEET POTATO FRIES is a collectible early learning book by Walter the Educator suitable for all ages belonging to Walter the Educator's Time to Eat Book Series. Collect more books at WaltertheEducator.com

USE THE EXTRA SPACE TO TAKE NOTES AND DOCUMENT YOUR MEMORIES

SWEET POTATO FRIES

Oh, it's time for a treat, a tasty surprise,

It's Time to Eat

Sweet Potato Fries

Golden and crispy, sweet potato fries!

Cut into sticks, so long and so thin,

Soft on the inside, with crunch to begin.

From the oven, they smell so sweet,

Warm and ready, oh, what a feat!

Sprinkled with salt, a pinch on top,

One bite, and it's hard to stop.

They're not too spicy, they're not too plain,

They're just the right mix, it's hard to explain!

Dipped in ketchup or left alone,

Sweet potato fries have a flavor all their own.

Orange like pumpkins, bright and fun,

.

Eating them feels like a day in the sun.

It's Time to Eat

Sweet Potato Fries

Crunch on the outside, soft in the heart,

Each little fry, a work of art!

They bring us smiles, so wide and bright,

Eating sweet fries just feels right.

Some like them with a dash of spice,

Or even with honey, oh, that's nice!

There's no wrong way to enjoy the fry,

With every taste, you'll want to sigh.

From dinner to lunch, a snack or more,

Sweet potato fries, we just adore.

They make us happy, they make us sing,

These yummy fries are the best thing!

So gather 'round and take a bite,

Golden orange, a yummy sight.

For early lunch or late night treat,

It's Time to Eat

Sweet Potato Fries

These fries are always fun to eat.

Let's share them with family, let's share with friends,

Sweet potato fries, the joy never ends!

One for me and one for you,

Each tasty fry feels fresh and new.

Now that you know, it's no surprise,

Nothing's better than sweet potato fries.

A treat so simple, a snack so neat,

Sweet potato fries can't be beat!

ABOUT THE CREATOR

Walter the Educator is one of the pseudonyms for Walter Anderson. Formally educated in Chemistry, Business, and Education, he is an educator, an author, a diverse entrepreneur, and he is the son of a disabled war veteran. "Walter the Educator" shares his time between educating and creating. He holds interests and owns several creative projects that entertain, enlighten, enhance, and educate, hoping to inspire and motivate you. Follow, find new works, and stay up to date with Walter the Educator™

at WaltertheEducator.com